Rails to the Lancashire

by

Richard Kirkman and Peter van Zeller

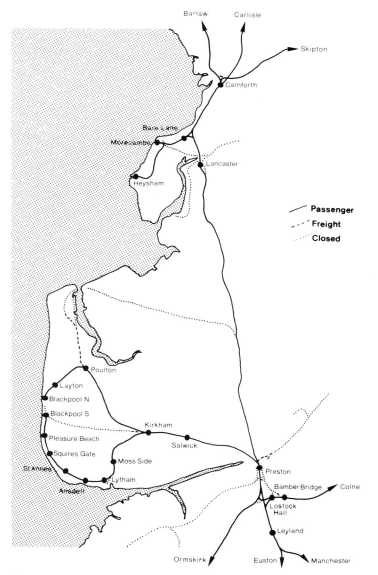

Passenger ——
Freight - - -
Closed ·····

AS the 150th Anniversaries of the Lancaster & Preston Junction and the Preston & Wyre Railways were celebrated in 1990, *Rails to the Lancashire Coast* was a suitable subject to follow our *Rails round the Cumbrian Coast*, published by Dalesman in 1988. Both these books give an illustrated account of railway development with detailed maps to identify abandoned trackbeds. The maps show the maximum extent of the rail network, as far as it can be ascertained, but not all features were present together. Route maps were drawn to a scale of 1 inch to 1 mile.

Those wishing to learn more should refer to Volume 10: The North West by G.O. Holt, revised by Gordon Biddle, in the *Regional History of the Railways of Great Britain* published by David & Charles. The Lancashire & Yorkshire Railway and the London & North Western Railway have specialist societies. Lancaster City Museum and the Harris Museum at Preston also have railway collections. Records can be found in local libraries, the Lancashire County Record Office at Preston, the Public Record Office at Kew and the National Railway Museum at York.

We would like to thank the staff of these organisations, the Preston Area Manager of British Rail and his staff, and the following individuals for their special help: Frank Dean, David Dixon, Neal Glover, John Hammond, David Joy, Jim Kay, Noel and Steven Machell, Peter W. Robinson, Nick Stanbra, Kate van Zeller and Graham Withers.

Dedicated to John McCullagh who taught the one-time station manager of Blackpool North how to manage a busy booking office.

Dalesman Publishing Co. Ltd.
Clapham, Lancaster LA2 2EB.
First published 1991
©Text Peter van Zeller 1991
©Maps Richard Kirkman 1991

Overleaf: ex LMS class 4 2-6-4T 42154 crossing Greyhound Bridge leaving Lancaster Green Ayre with the 13 53 Leeds-Morecambe on 12 June 1965 (photos: Noel A. Machell).

Printed by Smiths Colour Printers
Brighouse Road, Low Moor,
Bradford BD12 0NB

Lancaster Canal Tramroad

The names of the Old Tram Bridge over the Ribble and the Old Tramroad footpath recall the early plateway into Preston. The Lancaster Canal Company funds were low in 1803 when it built the five-mile tramroad to connect its northern section between Carnforth and Preston, and the southern section between Chorley and Wigan. Horses drew trains of six wagons on the double track, apart from the inclines at Avenham Park, Penwortham and Walton where there were endless chains driven by stationary engines. After the canal was completed to Kendal in 1819, the "temporary" tramroad continued in use for a further 60 years. It closed in stages from 1864 to 1879. A section of the cast-iron flanged rail, and a wheel from a runaway that plunged off the Avenham Incline into the river in 1826, are now displayed in the Harris Museum at Preston.

Preston

Rails to the Lancashire Coast

The narrow North Lancashire plain between the Pennine Hills and the Irish Sea is one of the thoroughfares of Britain. Before the Railway Age, the Lancashire coast was windswept and deserted. Where the road to Scotland bridged the River Lune at Lancaster and the Ribble at Preston the ancient ports were silting and in decline. When local interests built the railways from town to town, these short sections formed part of a network which brought great economic and social changes to the whole region. Old towns were revived, new harbours developed and a vast leisure industry grew beside the sea at the holiday resorts of Blackpool and Morecambe.

The first transport improvement in the region since the Roman roads was the opening of the Lancaster Canal in 1797 to carry coal north and lime south. After the Lune Aqueduct was built at Lancaster, funds were short, but a gap still lay in the route from Carnforth to the Leeds & Liverpool Canal at Wigan. To avoid flights of locks at the valley of the River Ribble, there was a double track tramroad at Preston. Trains were pulled by horses in a tunnel under Fishergate, across the Ribble on a trestle bridge, then climbed three steep inclines with endless chains driven by stationary steam engines.

This tramroad remained isolated, although visionaries did foresee the construction of a national network of railroads. In 1830 the young High Sheriff of Lancashire, Peter Hesketh, was a guest at the opening of the Liverpool & Manchester Railway. Having inherited the Rossall estate at the mouth of the Wyre and the family name of Fleetwood, he saw the opportunity for a new port linked to the ever lengthening chain of railways to the south.

The Wigan & Preston Railway, authorised on 22 April 1831, amalgamated with the Wigan Branch Railway to form the North Union Railway. Linked to the capital via the

One of the first six locomotives bought by the Lancaster & Preston Junction Railway. Bury 2-2-0 John o'Gaunt stands outside Lancaster Penny Street Station (print: J. Atherton courtesy of Lancaster City Museum).

L&MR, the Grand Junction and the London & Birmingham Railways, this had a commanding position when it opened in 1838. Its station at Preston was never bypassed and the site is still used today. While its own trains ran widely over other railways, it physically obstructed those of the Bolton & Preston Railway on which it had forced the link at Euxton Junction. Both lines soon came under a joint administration of the London & North Western and the Lancashire & Yorkshire Railways in 1847.

North of Preston three lines opened within weeks of each other. On 1 May 1840 the Preston & Longridge was only an isolated quarry railway, but the Lancaster & Preston Junction Railway opened with great aspirations on 25 June 1840 followed by the Preston & Wyre Railway on 15 July. The former was mainly promoted by citizens of Lancaster to ensure that their town was not bypassed by Joseph Locke's Grand Caledonian Junction Railway. It enjoyed the first royal journey by the Dowager Queen Adelaide in 1840 but alas soon became a shambles when the NUR stopped hiring locomotives and charged extortionate tolls for through trains using the connecting tunnel at Preston. The Lancaster Canal still prospered and turned the tables on its new competitor by leasing the L&PJR instead. It increased fares and even removed the seats on third class carriages to discourage their use!

Sir Peter Hesketh-Fleetwood promoted the Preston & Wyre Railway to make the mouth of the River Wyre "the most convenient and most economical channel leading to all the western parts of the world" — a haven he called Fleetwood. The major feature of the line was the two-mile timber trestle and embankment crossing the salt marshes north of Burn Naze. Any hope of land reclamation was dashed by the tides and another more circuitous line was laid along the shore. Although the P&WR connected with paddle steamers to Ardrossan, its part of the route from London to Scotland was not profitable. However in 1842 the line was approached by Sunday School managers to run an excursion that proved overwhelmingly popular. Soon so many passengers were walking to the coast at Blackpool that branch lines were opened in 1846 from Poulton to Blackpool

and Kirkham to Lytham. These lines also came under joint management by the Lancashire & Yorkshire and London & North Western Railways in 1847.

The position of the P&WR on the main route to Scotland did not last long as there were plans to build a railway north beyond Lancaster. Eminent engineers like George Stephenson and John Rastrick had surveyed routes across the tidal sands of Morecambe Bay, but they were rejected by a Government Commission in favour of a much shorter, steeper route through the fells. Joseph Locke laid out the Lancaster & Carlisle Railway along the upper part of the Lune valley, climbing at 1 in 74 to a summit at Shap. Sponsored by the lines to the south, it opened throughout on 15 December 1846 amid great controversy. It wanted to lease the L&PJR as did the East Lancashire Railway but the Lancaster Canal would not give up control. So the L&CR simply took free passage for its trains over the L&PJR — a practice which led to a collision and official pressure for the two companies to work with the London & North Western Railway which had now united the southern railways of the West Coast.

Meanwhile another North Western Railway had aimed to link Leeds and Scotland but only succeeded in building a line from Skipton via Lancaster to the coast of Morecambe Bay. Here another new port opened in 1849 but its proposed main line did not penetrate north of Ingleton against the opposition of the L&CR. The latter had also frustrated the Whitehaven & Furness Junction Extension Railway in its aim to link the Cumbrian Coast with West Yorkshire. Such links were not made until the Ulverstone & Lancaster Railway reached Carnforth in 1857, exhausted financially, and the Furness & Midland Joint Railway completed the line east to Wennington Junction in 1867.

At this period The Garstang & Knot-end Railway |sic| was promoted as the most direct route to Fleetwood but it took forty years, several Acts of Parliament and new companies to complete its twelve-mile track. Despite such aspirations it was never more than a country byway, like the Blackpool & Lytham Railway, which opened in 1863 but remained completely isolated until 1874.

LANCASHIRE &
YORKSHIRE
RAILWAY

THIS IS
THE
LINE
WE'RE
GOING BY
TO
BLACKPOOL

BLACKPOOL LOOKING NORTH.

Top left: *L&YR "High Flier" 4-4-2 with a Manchester-Blackpool express has just taken water on the Down Fast line at Lea Road troughs, circa 1902 (photo: P. van Zeller collection).*
Bottom left: *Rails were the arteries of Blackpool; both North and Central stations can be seen from the air, while countless trams pick their way through the crowds on the promenade (photo: R. Kirkman collection).*
Opposite top: *The first experiments in high voltage AC electrification took place at Morecambe with this Westinghouse-built Midland Railway motor coach and its innovatory pantograph at Promenade station in 1909 (photo: R. Kirkman collection).*

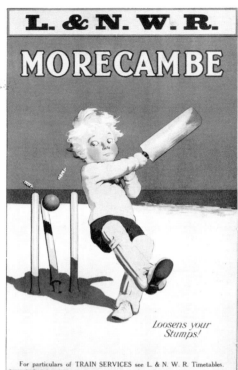

As the suburban development of Blackpool increased rapidly, a new Blackpool Railway was promoted to link with the West Lancashire and the Manchester, Sheffield & Lincolnshire Railways. In 1885 the town led the world by building an electric tramway along the seafront. The electrical supply hidden in an underground conduit was susceptible to sea water but the Blackpool Electric Tramway Company led directly to the development of vast urban tram networks in the following two decades. North from Talbot Square station another line opened in 1898, the Blackpool & Fleetwood Tramroad. Like an American Interurban railway this was built through the countryside on its own right-of-way. It still runs through the suburbs it generated and terminates at Fleetwood on the last section of traditional street tramway in Britain.

Lancaster and the new borough of Morecambe also laid a tramway network, although there were separate systems with overhead trolley wires for Lancaster, horses for the route to Morecambe and the seafront line which eventually was worked by petrol trams. In competition, the Midland Railway chose here to test its proposals to electrify the Derby-Manchester main line. In 1908 the line from its new port of Heysham to Morecambe and Lancaster was the first British use of alternating current. Although the Lancashire & Yorkshire Railway electrified its line to Southport, the Joint line to Blackpool was improved to handle the ever growing holiday traffic by steam. In 1903 a new line was built from a flyover at Kirkham to shorten the southerly route into Blackpool Central. On the Fylde the L&YR used track circuits and intermediate block signals between signal boxes with Train Control from Manchester, to further increase the capacity of "The Business Line" at peak holiday periods.

Meanwhile the London & North Western Railway regarded itself as "The Premier Line" — by 1879 it owned the route from Euston to Carlisle apart from the short section from Euxton Junction to Preston held jointly with the L&YR. Close co-operation between the two led to their amalgamation just before the main grouping of 1923, when they were joined by the Midland and the Garstang & Knott End in the London, Midland & Scottish Railway. Yet by 1930 bus competition led to most stations closing to passengers between Preston and Lancaster, and on the branches to Glasson Dock, Knott End and Longridge.

Throughout this period Preston remained an important point on the West Coast Main Line where trains combined or changed engines and crews. Although trains no longer had a lunch stop, expresses ran to London, Birmingham, Liverpool, Manchester, Barrow, Workington, Windermere, Edinburgh and Glasgow. Long after the Second World War the holiday traffic to Blackpool was hauled by steam traction. Then as the British Railways Modernisation plan proposed widespread main-line electrification, to test the new high-voltage AC systems the Lancaster-Morecambe-Heysham electric line was converted to 6,600V ac 50 cycles. However, its new station opened in 1957 at Scale Hall did not even survive ten years.

In 1962 the Beeching Plan recommended removal of all duplicating routes and stations. At Blackpool, closure of North station was proposed with traffic being taken to Central. In the event Central was closed along with the New line, North was left as the main station while the loop through Lytham was cut back to Blackpool South and now survives as a basic railway without sidings.

At Morecambe, Euston Road station was an early victim, although the Lancaster-Morecambe-Heysham electrics soon followed in 1966 along with the rest of the Lune Valley line to Wennington. Trains from Leeds were diverted via Carnforth. Although there were thoughts of linking Bare Lane to the Heysham line, trains to the port continued to

Opposite top: LMS Class 5 4-6-0 5230 leaves Blackpool Central with a train for Colne. The site became a vast car park where the platform edges could be seen 25 years after closure (photo: Frank Dean).
Opposite bottom: BR Class 142 at Blackpool South with a train for Colne in 1990. The route of the Marton line to Kirkham is followed by the motorway link road in the background (photo: P. van Zeller).
Right: BR Class 90 propels a Glasgow-London express past Oubeck loops 150 years after the L&PJR main line opened (photo: R. Kirkman).

reverse at Promenade. However, a decline in traffic to Belfast after the Troubles led to the withdrawal of ferry services and the last Belfast Boat Train in 1973.

Meanwhile, three depots in the North West were the last to keep steam locomotives until August 1968, then the main line lost all its intermediate stations and goods yards. After years of indecision, the West Coast main line electrification was finally completed north of Preston in 1974, when Queen Elizabeth II took another royal train journey in the cab of an electric locomotive.

However, electrification of the routes to Blackpool, Liverpool and Manchester, to allow through running without engine changes at Preston, was not deemed commercially viable in 1985. Instead, the introduction of Sprinter Express services to the Provincial sector made Blackpool a terminal for trains across country as far away as Harwich. It also remains an important Intercity destination from London, with Regional Railways services from Stockport and Manchester. From 1989 these were marketed as part of Network North West.

Local freight survived with chemical traffic from ICI at Burn Naze, bulk coal deliveries to Deepdale, oil to Preston Dock, and irradiated nuclear fuel from Heysham. Carnforth retained its sidings mainly for permanent way vehicles. The ports created by the railways, and much of the track mileage, have survived and adapted to the changing economy of the region. Lancaster and Preston continue to thrive and to enjoy a fast service to the capital, because of the railways promoted by their citizens in the 1830s, while the urban development of the Fylde has exceeded the wildest dreams of Peter Hesketh-Fleetwood.

Although there have been many changes through rationalisation and modernisation, the present rail routes to the Lancashire Coast still reveal their past history in station architecture, track layouts, train services, and all the fixtures and fittings along the route. Even the mile posts north of Preston still mark the territories of the Lancaster & Preston Junction and the Preston & Wyre Railways 150 years after their opening in 1840.

Trains to the Lancashire Coast

The North Union Railway ran trains for its neighbours with four-wheeled Bury-type locomotives until they acquired similar machines capable of 40 mph although they could barely stop a light load. The first train opening the Lancaster & Preston Junction Railway would not start due to "the newness of the machinery" and had to be double-headed. Some Fleetwood excursions had 55 coaches behind two engines. Often trains needed a push from the porters to get going through the Fishergate Tunnel at Preston!

The Lancaster & Carlisle required motive power of a different order to climb Shap, and was originally worked by LNWR locomotives of the Crewe 2-2-2 and 2-4-0 types. These were scheduled to run on expresses at an average of 30 mph while goods trains were to run at 12 mph. The surviving 1847 2-2-2 *Cornwall* with its huge 8-ft driving wheels regularly worked the Mail from Crewe to Carlisle.

As the LNWR developed Crewe works and the L&YR established Horwich, they built locomotives which were as subtly different as their black liveries. Both lines depended on fleets of 0-6-0s for goods. Although the LNWR under Francis Webb used its compound 2-2-2-2s on expresses over Shap, it was the simple 2-4-0s which did the most useful work, like the surviving *Hardwicke* that ran to Carlisle at an average 67.2 mph in the 1895 Races.

The L&YR developed Atlantic 4-4-2s with such big driving wheels they became known as Highfliers, and followed with the four-cylinder Dreadnought 4-6-0s. Meanwhile the Midland stayed with relatively small four-coupled passenger locomotives and six-coupled goods engines, although examples of its American 2-6-0s were seen in Lancaster. It introduced steam railmotors from Lancaster to Heysham before electrification — one survived as a saloon to become preserved in the National Collection.

In the traditions of their smaller locomotives, the later LNWR 4-4-0 and 4-6-0s were thrashed — one was blamed for setting fire to Lighthouse signal box near Lytham in 1912 as "L&YR locomotives did not throw sparks!" However, the great processions of trains to Blackpool always included

many small 2-4-2 tanks and 0-6-0 coal engines which could and did keep express schedules with their heavy loads.

An early development from the co-operation between the L&YR and LNWR locomotive departments was the introduction of the L&YR Dreadnought 4-6-0s onto the West Coast Main Line. However, rebuilt with Walschaert's valve gear like the latest LNWR Claughtons, they were still no match for the Great Western Railway 4-6-0 *Launceston Castle* during trials before the construction of the Royal Scot class in 1927. The Scots could perform feats over Shap far beyond the LMS 4-4-0s of Midland origins, but one of the latter ran the first non-stop from London to Glasgow.

The new Stanier locomotives were not an instant success — the Jubilees were deemed less dependable by Blackpool crews than the old Dreadnoughts or their preferred Patriots. The 4-6-2 Princess Royals were distinctly winded at first by the non-stop runs to Carlisle. Not so the blue streamlined Coronation class 4-6-2s introduced to work the Coronation Scot, and the non-streamlined Duchesses. LNER engines were a rare sight before nationalisation, but thereafter B1s, K1s and occasional Pacifics were seen on through trains to Blackpool and excursions. The final "Lanky" Dreadnought ran its last trains in 1951.

Top: *LNWR Precursor 4-4-0 with a Scotch express of West Coast Joint Stock near Galgate around 1910. (photo: Sir Aubrey Brocklebank).*

Bottom: *LMS 6P Patriot class 4-6-0 and ex LNWR 0-8-0 8909 make an unlikely pair to double head a Warrington-Blackpool Central train at Preston in August 1938. The fireman of the goods loco has made full steam while his colleague on the Patriot can relax and chat (photo: Frank Dean).*

Opposite: *L&YR 4-4-2 1395 pauses at Ansdell. When built in 1899, it was "the mightiest express loco ... with the largest boiler on a British railway" (photo: P. van Zeller collection).*

A harbinger of the future was the operation in 1928 of a four-car diesel-electric train between Blackpool and Preston. Some innovative locomotives were built at the Dick Kerr works of English Electric including some railcars for Bermuda, with two 150hp engines, epicyclic gearboxes and shaft drive. Predecessors of the BR Diesel Multiple Unit, they were tested on the Longridge line. Various designs of diesel shunter developed into the BR Class 08, and later the prototype Deltic was built at Preston. DMUs began to work services to Blackpool where a fueling plant was sited at Central just before closure.

Meanwhile the Stanier 4-6-2s were put out to grass as their main line work was taken over by English Electric type 4s

Below: *Ex LMS 4-6-2 46243 City of Lancaster passes through Bolton-le-Sands with a Glasgow-Birmingham train on 27 April 1958. This loco has the sloping smokebox top from when it was the last of the class to remain streamlined (photo: Noel A. Machell).*
Opposite top: *An Anglo-Scottish express headed by BR English Electric D404 south as far as Crewe. Preston No 3 box in 1970 controlled the East Lancs junction (photo: P. van Zeller).*
Opposite bottom: *20 years later at the same point, a Driving Van Trailer heads a southbound electric express. The East Lancs sidings had become a carpark, while the colour light signals are worked from the Powerbox (photo: P. van Zeller).*

later designated Class 40s. On secondary trains, Britannia Class 4-6-2s and other BR Standard and Stanier locomotives ran until the end of steam in 1967. However, before schedules improved greatly, the West Coast Main Line had to await the Class 50s, which from 1970 ran locals to Carlisle or double-headed on heavy trains to Glasgow.

After electrification throughout London-Glasgow trains only changed crews at Preston, however the battering of axle-hung motors damaged the track newly relaid with limestone ballast and hastened the rebuilding of Class 86 locomotives. Blackpool trains now change engines at Preston, although the once ubiquitous Class 40s have been long outlived by Class 47s. Yet only rarely have electric multiple units ever penetrated to Lancaster and beyond.

From 1980, the West Coast Main Line was used to test the ability of the prototype Advanced Passenger Trains to tilt at high speeds on the sharp curves where the North Union met the Liverpool & Manchester at Golborne and on Joseph Locke's sinuous route from Lancaster Old Junction to Glasgow. Alas the train only managed a few days of public service before bequeathing its livery to BR Intercity. Subsequently stretches of the main line were designated for 110 mph running by Class 87 and 86/2s. These types also work in multiple on heavy Freightliner trains. Although the Class 89 was tested on Shap, where poor rail conditions still cause adhesion problems, new Class 90 locomotives were introduced in 1989. The silent start of trains now propelled with Driving Van Trailers is in stark contrast to earlier traction. The InterCity 250 train announced in 1990 for the West Coast Main Line was to follow this push-pull formation.

On secondary services, all types of modern multiple units are found. Class 142 Pacers appeared in various liveries including Provincial Blue and Manchester Passenger Transport Executive Brown, and even brown and cream recalling earlier Great Western through excursions to Blackpool. Class 150 Sprinters in Network North West, Class 155 and 158s in West Yorkshire red, 156 and 158s in blue make the North West as colourful as at any time since the bright yellow coaches of the first trains.

Lancaster

Longridge

Ribbleton

Red Scar Works

Tramway

Blackpool

Oxheys

Deepdale Mill St

Greenbank Siding

Deepdale St

Goods

Preston Dock

Maudland

PRESTON

Fishergate Avenham Incline

Ribble Jn

N

Penwortham Jn Whitehouse Jns

W

Middleforth Jn S

Cop Lane Penwortham Incline

Skew Bridge

Farington Curve Jn **Preston Junction** Bamber Bridge Jn

BAMBER BRIDGE Blackburn

New Longton & Hutton

Southport **LOSTOCK HALL**

Moss Lane Jn East Jn Tramway

Farington

Farington Jn Walton Summit

Ormskirk ↓ Crewe

"Proud Preston"

For centuries "Proud Preston" has commanded the lowest crossing of the River Ribble and was a major commercial centre long before the Railway Age. Half way between London and Glasgow, it became a great railway junction, although it had no company workshops like Crewe. Preston is at the hub of tracks to north and south along the West Coast Main Line, east to Blackburn and Leeds, south-east to Bolton and Manchester, south-west to Liverpool and north-west to Blackpool. Only byways like the West Lancashire direct route to Southport and part of the Longridge branch have been closed and lifted.

The complex of junctions south of the town resulted from the intense competition between rival companies when these lines were built. First into Preston, the North Union Railway opened on 31 October 1838 extending a chain of railways that started in London. This gave it the financial power to impose on the lines that followed.

The next on the scene, the Bolton & Preston Railway, leased the Lancaster Canal Company's tramroad with the aim of using that route into the town. However, the NUR objected to the B&PR offering a shorter journey from Manchester and forced it to join NUR tracks into Preston at Euxton Junction in 1843. When B&PR trains were obstructed by the NUR, they used road coaches into Preston. The two companies did agree to amalgamate, but within 18 months were leased jointly by the London & North Western and the Lancashire & Yorkshire Railways. At length in 1888, the main line south of Euxton Junction became London & North Western Railway, from Bolton to Euxton became Lancashire & Yorkshire Railway and from Euxton to Preston station a Joint line with profits shared 60-34!

The East Lancashire Railway first bypassed the town on its main route from Blackburn to Liverpool via Ormskirk. Its trains to Preston had to reverse at Farington, but the ELR was provoked by the NUR into the vast expense of building its own line into the town over the immense 52-arch Ribble viaduct. Later a series of curves joined the ELR where it crossed over the West Coast Main Line which Blackburn trains now use from Farington Curve Junction after the East Lancs Preston Extension closed in 1972.

Finally the West Lancashire Railway had its own bridge over the Ribble to a remote terminus opened for the 1882 Preston Guild. In 1900 Whitehouse curve linked it to the East Lancs route into Preston and the Fishergate Hill station became a goods yard until 1965.

These curves allowed trains to take many permutations of route. Going from the north via the East Lancs station, Preston Junction and Farington Curve Junction, a Blackpool train would pass through Preston twice!

Ribble Viaduct

The first North Union Railway bridge is the east side of a complex structure. Its five 120-ft arches still carry the bi-directional fast lines. It was widened by 1880 to carry the slow and up goods lines. Downstream, lattice girders of 1900 carry the down goods and shunting line to the Docks Branch and what is still North Union Yard.

To the east stands the East Lancs bridge. The ELR was obliged to landscape the river bank to gain the consent of Preston Corporation to build its independent access to the town. Flooding in 1849 brought down 13 of the 52 arches before the line opened, and 48 arches were filled in to make the long embankment which now stands unused.

Preston Dock

The branch descending at 1 in 29 in the midst of the yard was a joint North Union Railway and Ribble Navigation Company venture. The Ribble Branch Railway opened in 1846 to ship Wigan coal from Victoria Quay. Preston Corporation acquired the Navigation and opened the Albert Edward Dock in July 1892. One of its steam shunting locomotives, *Princess*, now operates on the Lakeside & Haverthwaite Railway in Cumbria. Sidings led to the Dick, Kerr & Co works which made more tramcars than any other firm in Britain. As part of English Electric, it followed with the prototype Deltic in 1961. Although the docks closed to commercial shipping in 1981, the railway was relaid along a new route with sidings to Lancashire Tar Distillers, Petrofina and an award-winning engine shed.

Top left: *LNWR Claughton 4-6-0 with a down Scotch Express nears Preston by Farington Curve Junction.*

Bottom left: *L&YR 2-4-2 radial tank 1318 on a Blackpool-Manchester via Atherton train at Farington. This was the most numerous class of 358 built at Horwich between 1889 and 1911 (photos: R. Kirkman collection).*

Opposite top right: *The lattice girders extended the original North Union bridge over the Ribble. Beyond is the original East Lancs bridge (photo: P. van Zeller collection).*

Opposite top left: *Bagnall 0-6-0ST Perseverance with a RCTS Railtour at Preston Dock on 4 May 1960.*

Opposite bottom: *ex LMS 4-6-0 45545 passing North Union Yard on 15 October 1963. The track behind the loco fell towards Preston Dock. The name "Planet" recalls that Liverpool & Manchester Railway trains ran to Preston at the start of NUR services in 1838 (photos: Noel A. Machell).*

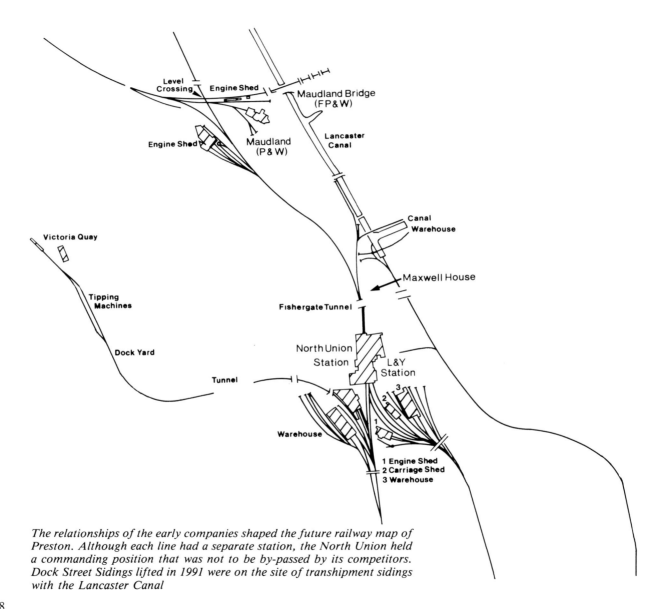

Level Crossing
Engine Shed
Maudland Bridge (FP&W)
Engine Shed
Maudland (P&W)
Lancaster Canal
Canal Warehouse
Victoria Quay
Maxwell House
Tipping Machines
Fishergate Tunnel
Dock Yard
North Union Station
L&Y Station
Tunnel
3
2
Warehouse
1
1 Engine Shed
2 Carriage Shed
3 Warehouse

The relationships of the early companies shaped the future railway map of Preston. Although each line had a separate station, the North Union held a commanding position that was not to be by-passed by its competitors. Dock Street Sidings lifted in 1991 were on the site of transhipment sidings with the Lancaster Canal

Preston Station

The 1838 North Union Railway station had its buildings each side of the tracks with their turntables for hand shunting coaches. It was linked by a narrow tunnel under Fishergate to the Lancaster & Preston Junction Railway. To avoid a tunnel toll of 6d, through passengers would get out to walk across the road and rebook, but often found their "connecting train" had already left early!

The station was highly regarded at first but it was swamped by the growth of traffic through "the busiest station in the land". In 1850 East Lancashire Railway tracks joined at the south end, but there was no foot-bridge and passengers just wandered over the rails. As the various companies argued about improvements, part of the roof fell down in 1866, and it was described as "the most dismal, dilapidated, disgraceful looking station in Christendom!" Before West Coast Main Line expresses had dining cars, through trains stopped for fifteen minutes while "a hot and perspiring woman" carved lunch.

The current station resulted from a £250,000 rebuilding in 1877-80 when a bridge replaced the tunnel, and the main Fishergate entrance led on to the great island platform 1,225 ft long and 100 ft wide beneath a new roof. There was a Post Office sorting depot, above the extensive dining rooms where the "Preston Ordinary" was now served by waitresses "overflowing with attention"!

Further improvements were awaiting royal assent when there was disaster on the sharp curve beyond Fishergate. After a period of racing with the East Coast railways to Aberdeen, a 10 mph speed limit was misjudged by the drivers of the 8pm down Highland Express. At 40mph they derailed, scattering wreckage and killing a passenger — the Railway Races to the North stopped forthwith!

The Dock Street Viaduct was then widened to allow six roads north on a gentler curve and in 1903 a new island platform was also added. Although the East Lancashire was taken over by the Lancashire & Yorkshire Railway in 1859, its name stuck to the eastern platforms, which had their own station master and gained a new entrance on Butler Street in the 1900s. Preston remained virtually unchanged until that route closed on 1 May 1972 for the area to become a carpark.

Only in 1885 was Maudland Bridge station closed, the flat crossings removed from the West Coast Main Line and the curve from the Longridge line built into Preston station. The alignment of sidings and goods shed still indicated the old FP&WRJR route in 1991 when a platform was briefly reinstated during bridge renewals.

Preston shed was on the west side of the main line. It was developed by the London & North Western Railway and remained almost unchanged until it suffered fire in 1960 and was demolished in 1966. The Power Signalling Centre adjacent to the site was completed in 1973 and replaced many boxes on the main line alone.

Elsewhere, tracks like the mid-platform crossovers which enabled trains to be split or combined, were simplified; resignalling removed the old semaphore signal gantries; and electrification brought yet another change to the Preston railway scene in 1973.

Maudlands Junction

North of Preston the junctions were on the level but the relationships of the railways were far from it. Tracks in front of Ladywell House, the area offices, served the Lancaster Canal basin before it was filled in. Here the Bolton & Preston Railway briefly had its Maxwell House station unconnected to its own tracks but used by the Lancaster & Preston Junction Railway during confrontations with the NUR. But the L&PJR had received its own royal assent after the Preston & Wyre Railway which had planned a station at Maudlands. The L&PJR had to cross this in order to link with the NUR and inevitably there were accidents. On 18 September 1845 a Fleetwood excursion train with goods trucks full of passengers was cut in two by an express from Lancaster, yet no one was killed. Close by another flat crossing later linked the P&WR to the Fleetwood, Preston & West Riding Junction Railway which despite its name was only a mile long!

Top: *Half a million people used the original North Union station during the week of the 1862 Preston Guild. Passengers wandered across the track as there was no footbridge. The roof partly collapsed before the station was completely rebuilt in 1879 (photo: Harris Museum & Art Gallery).*
Bottom: *BR Class 47 hauls the 12-50 from Blackpool into Preston from where an electric loco will propel the train to Euston. The magnificent 1879 centre island platform buildings still support a trainshed decorated with wrought-iron "roses" (photo: R. Kirkman).*

At Preston ex L&YR Aspinall 4-4-0 10179 and 2-4-2T 10820 have taken over a Barrow-Blackpool Central train from ex Furness Railway locos. Across the platform ex L&YR 2-4-2T 10847 waits with a Blackburn train for the same destination in August 1927 (photo: Frank Dean).

Top: *ex LMS Class 5 4-6-0 45473 leaves Preston with a Blackpool train in 1967. In the distance beyond Fishergate viaduct, Preston No 4 box had 170 levers (photo: P. van Zeller).*

Bottom: *BR Class 4 4-6-0 75017 at Maudlands Junction with the 6pm Blackpool Central to Southport on 31 August 1963. The warehouse behind the loco stands on the original Preston & Wyre terminus site. The dangerous flat crossings lasted here until the curve to the Longridge branch was added in 1885 (photo: Frank Dean).*

Ex LMS Class 5 4-6-0 44729 pulls the 11-35 Summer Saturdays train from Blackpool to Newcastle off the Up Fast at Maudlands Junction. This train was scheduled to run through Preston twice using curves south of the station to avoid the delay of a loco change in the platforms. L&PJR sleeper blocks were used in the construction of the spire of St Walburge (photo: John M. Hammond).

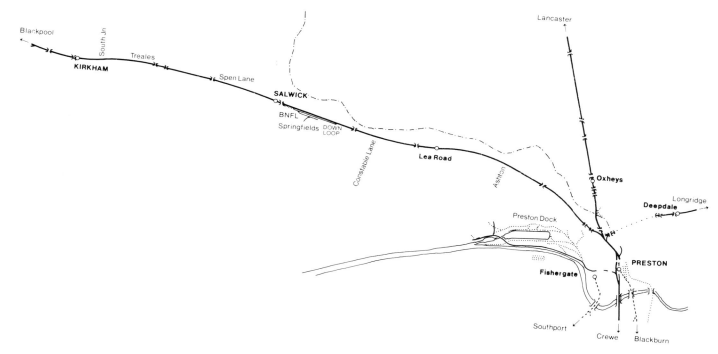

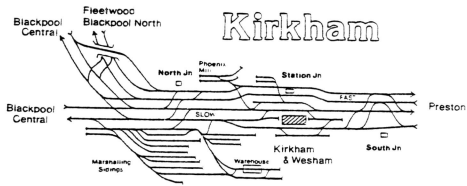

Kirkham

Lea Road and Salwick Stations

When the Preston & Wyre Railway opened in 1840, the Fylde was all as rural as it remains north of Lea Road, sited near malt kilns on the Lancaster Canal. Rising passenger traffic led to the track being doubled in 1846 and branch lines being built to the coast. Lea Road was close to a proposed junction for an extension of the Lancaster & Carlisle Railway to bypass the Lancaster & Preston Junction Railway when it was under lease to the Canal. Then, in a turmoil of railway politics in 1849, the P&WR was taken over by the Lancashire & Yorkshire Railway with a third share vested in the London & North Western Railway. Within thirty years, traffic had grown at such a rate that the Joint line was choked and a new Blackpool Railway was promoted in 1884 to give an independent route which it was expected that the Manchester, Sheffield & Lincolnshire Railway would build and operate.

Instead the existing track was quadrupled from Preston to Kirkham in 1889 and several stations were rebuilt by the L&YR with island platforms on the slow lines. Lea Road and Salwick had similar layouts with access from under and overbridge respectively. Both stations closed in 1938, but Salwick reopened and had sidings into the nearby Springfields plant of British Nuclear Fuels Ltd. Salwick No 2 was a fringe box where trains passed from the Preston panel to the manual boxes which continued to serve the Fylde in 1991. The Lea Road water troughs were sited on all four tracks between the two stations until the fast lines were taken out after 14 November 1965.

Kirkham & Wesham Station

In 1991 the only remaining section of four tracks on the main line passed through Kirkham & Wesham station, where the single track diverged for Lytham. This branch had opened on 16 February 1846 but the junction was then further from Preston with a sharp curve on to the main line. A platform at the old Lytham Junction itself soon closed in 1853, but through coaches were shunted here on to main line trains until 1 July 1874. A new direct cut off was then opened from Wrea Green to Kirkham on the present alignment, while the old line remained as the Bradkirk siding, the route of which can still be traced.

When the track to Preston was quadrupled in 1889 the present station at Kirkham & Wesham was built on the slow lines. Then as the Lancashire Wakes holiday traffic continued to grow, a brand new 6¾-mile direct line was built from Kirkham to Blackpool South Shore to give even more capacity for trains. This reduced the distance to Central station by 5½ miles, while to ease problems at the junction for the various routes, a flyover was built from the up Blackpool direct line to the up main line.

After this was completed in 1903, the Kirkham signal boxes were incredibly busy — Kirkham South Junction box sorted trains first for the station or the through fast lines, then Kirkham North Junction box directed them to one of the three routes into Blackpool. With all its 75 levers fully operational, this box handled a record 656 trains past here in a single day in August 1936.

When the direct line finally closed to excursions in 1967, the flyover was removed leaving only an abutment. The former down line towards Central still diverges for Kirkham Tip — the Area Maintenance Engineer's site for tipping spent ballast. Beyond this the trackbed of the direct line was used for the M55 motorway. By 1982 the line to Blackpool South had become a basic railway, with diesel multiple units on a shuttle service from Kirkham. This station lost its canopy but retained its buildings. Wrea Green and Moss Side stations both closed in 1961; yet while the former vanished completely, the latter was reopened in 1983 next to the open automatic crossing.

Opposite top: *Ex L&YR rebuilt 4-6-0 with the Manchester Victoria to Blackpool "Club" train ran 52 miles in 75 minutes non stop to Lytham. The train is on the Down Fast on the quadruple track near Spen Lane (photo: P. van Zeller collection).*

Opposite bottom: *Hughes 4-6-4 T 11114 with a Blackpool Central to Manchester Victoria crossing the Kirkham Flying Junction from the Up Marton-line in August 1939. Although the bridge has gone, the Down line to the left still serves sidings at Kirkham tip (photo: Frank Dean).*

Top: *The last L&YR "Dreadnought" 4-6-0 10442 with an up freight at Kirkham North Junction in August 1949. The Up line from the Flyover joined the line from Poulton by the signal box (photo: Frank Dean).*

Bottom: *BR Class 40 126 passes the same place with a Blackpool North-London Euston train in 1983. The flyover has been removed but the trackbed can still be seen opposite the then double track connection to Blackpool South (photo: R. Kirkman).*

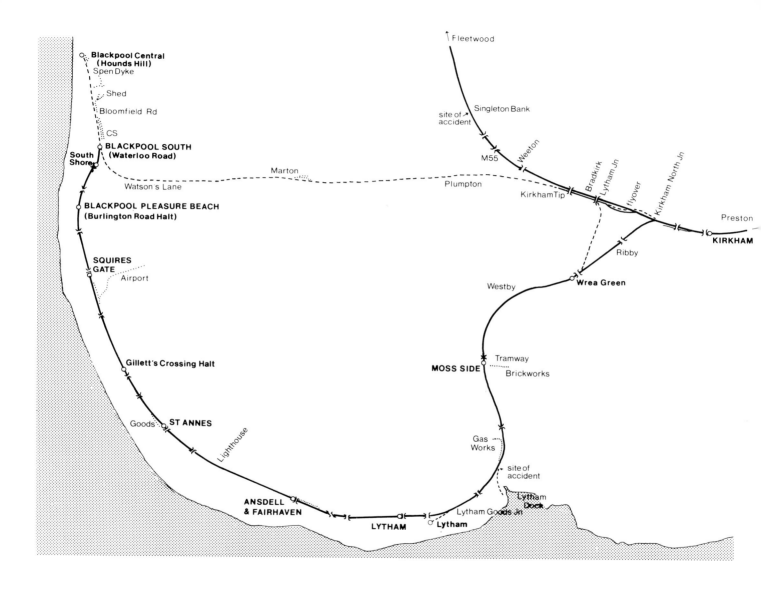

Blackpool Central
(Hounds Hill)
Spen Dyke
Shed
Bloomfield Rd
CS
BLACKPOOL SOUTH
(Waterloo Road)
South Shore
BLACKPOOL PLEASURE BEACH
(Burlington Road Halt)
SQUIRES GATE
Airport
Gillett's Crossing Halt
Goods   ST ANNES
Lighthouse
ANSDELL & FAIRHAVEN
LYTHAM
Lytham
Lytham Goods Jn
Lytham Dock
site of accident
Gas Works
MOSS SIDE   Tramway
Brickworks
Westby   Wrea Green
Ribby
Watson's Lane
Marton
Plumpton
KirkhamTip
Bradkirk
Lytham Jn
flyover
Kirkham North Jn
Preston
KIRKHAM
M55
Weeton
Singleton Bank
site of accident
Fleetwood

28

Lytham Station

The Preston & Wyre Railway opened its branch in 1846 to Lytham's original station which survived for goods until 1963. A branch to Lytham Dock had its own station from 1865 to 1874. Pointwork into sidings here was the factor which caused a tyre to shatter on a Lancashire & Yorkshire 4-4-0 locomotive in 1924 causing a major derailment. Adjacent to nearby Lytham Creek, the Lytham Motive Power Museum has laid a short 1ft 10¾ in gauge track.

From 1863 the independent Lytham & Blackpool Railway ran to Hounds Hill on a completely isolated route until it was absorbed by the P&WR in 1871. A half-mile link between the two sections was opened on 1 July 1874 with a new station. Its classical buildings "resembled a well kept conservatory" and as a pub have survived, whereas the bay platform for the Blackpool motor trains did not.

Ansdell & Fairhaven Station

The Fylde coastline was a sandy rabbit warren when this station opened in 1872. A century later when the island platform buildings were demolished, much of the area was covered in housing developed by the Fairhaven Estate. A Hudswell Clark 0-4-0 was used in construction work but the engine and its track went to the Western Front in 1915.

St Annes-on-the-Sea Station

First opened in November 1873 as Cross Slack, this was renamed St Annes in 1875. Efficient transport to the Lancashire hinterland made daily commuting possible and encouraged the growth of dormitory suburbs. In 1895 the Lytham, St Annes and Blackpool Travelling Club persuaded the Lancashire & Yorkshire Railway to build two private Club coaches. They were attached to the Manchester train and only the 50 subscribing members travelled in their reserved seats, with all windows closed by Club rules!

St Annes-on-the-Sea was rebuilt in 1926 with longer platforms and a bay facing Blackpool. Freight traffic ceased in 1968. Then the structures on the down platform were demolished in 1983 to make way for a supermarket, being replaced by a small modern building while the disused up platform awnings decayed further.

Squires Gate Station

A station was provided at Stoney Hill on 1 April 1865 which closed in 1872. The current station opened nearby on 14 September 1931 to serve the new airport which had a long private siding. Squires Gate still advertises Rail-Air Interchange for flights to the Isle of Man.

Pleasure Beach Station

Ground-level halts were opened in 1913 at Burlington Road and Gillett's Crossing Halt when steam rail-motors were introduced between Blackpool Central and Lytham. Although both closed in 1939, Burlington Road reopened as Pleasure Beach in April 1987. On the Pleasure Beach itself a 21-in gauge miniature railway was laid in 1934.

Blackpool South Station

The single-track stub and its platform are the remnants of Waterloo Road station, where the new direct line from Kirkham joined the old route from Lytham. The road which now sweeps alongside from the M55 motorway follows the track bed of the direct line, which had opened in 1903 and closed in 1964. The platform which remains was added along the Lytham line on 14 July 1916 to replace the old South Shore station. It was renamed Blackpool South in March 1932, and became a terminus in place of Blackpool Central in 1965. By 1982 only a single track survived.

Beyond the long overbridge behind the station, no less than 34 parallel tracks ran towards Blackpool Central. This had opened in 1863 as Hounds Hill, but was completely rebuilt by Easter 1901 with new entrance buildings and 1½ miles of platforms, six covered and eight open for excursion trains. When Central closed the platforms were infilled to allow car parking and could still be seen in 1991.

Top: *L&YR 4-4-2 No 1392 leaves Ansdell with a train for Lytham (photo: P. van Zeller collection).*

Bottom: *ex L&YR 4-4-2 10307 at St Annes-on-the-Sea in April 1933 with a Blackpool Central-Liverpool Exchange train. In 1991 the platform and awning behind the loco survived without tracks (photo: Frank Dean).*

Opposite top: *Ex MR 0-4-4T 1340 with an Illuminations Shuttle push/pull train to St Annes in September 1928. Gilletts Crossing Halt vanished after 1939 (photo: Frank Dean).*

Opposite bottom left: *Blackpool Pleasure Beach Railway with the original 4-6-4T Carol Jean of 1934.*

Opposite bottom right: *A 15-in gauge railway ran at St Annes from 1956 to 1961. The diesel electric loco Princess Anne was built by Barlows in Southport (photos: R. Kirkman).*

The Miniature Railway, St Annes-on-the

Top: *Blackpool Central awaits returning visitors with over 80 coaches in the platforms. The pennies from the toilets (which still stand) were reputed to pay the rates bill for the station! (photo: Evening Gazette).*

Bottom: *Swansong at Blackpool Central on 7 July 1963. As ex LMS Class 5 44927 arrives from Manchester Victoria, Jubilee 45653 Barham leaves with a train for Leeds City which includes an ex LNER artic set, while another four trains are also waiting to depart (photo: Frank Dean).*

Opposite top: *ex LMS Class 5 45241 leaves Blackpool South with a Wigan train on 19 July 1961. The Marton line curved in from the right but only Platform 1 survives today (photo: Frank Dean).*

Opposite bottom: *The last days of Blackpool South in 1982 before the branch was singled first to St Annes and then to Kirkham. Rationalisation already meant that the signalman could not see any trains from the box! (photo: Nick Stanbra).*

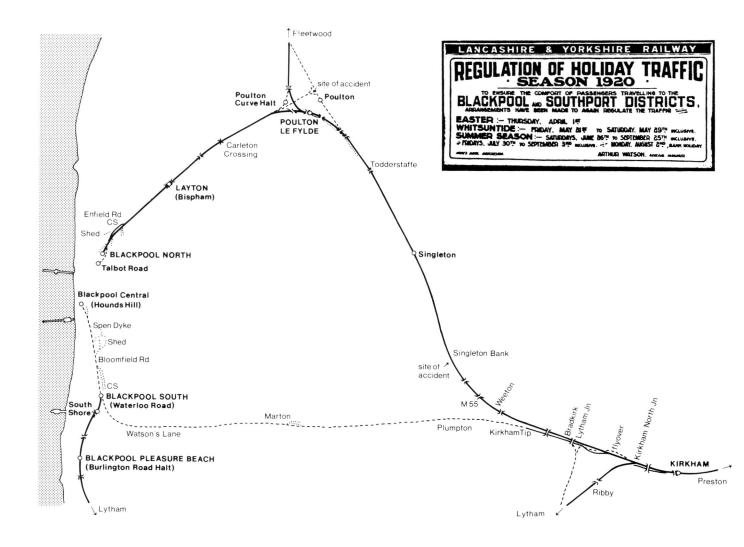

↑ Fleetwood

site of accident
Poulton
Poulton
Curve Halt
POULTON
LE FYLDE

Carleton
Crossing

Todderstaffe

LAYTON
(Bispham)

Enfield Rd
CS
Shed

BLACKPOOL NORTH
Talbot Road

Singleton

Blackpool Central
(Hounds Hill)

Spen Dyke

Shed

Bloomfield Rd

Singleton Bank

site of
accident

M 55   Weeton

CS

BLACKPOOL SOUTH
(Waterloo Road)

South
Shore

Marton

Plumpton

Watson's Lane

Kirkham Tip

Bradkirk
Lytham Jn
Flyover
Kirkham North Jn

KIRKHAM

BLACKPOOL PLEASURE BEACH
(Burlington Road Halt)

Preston

Ribby

↘ Lytham

Lytham

Singleton and Weeton

A station opened at Weeton in 1870 and closed on 2 May 1932. On 16 July 1961, an accident occurred with a Diesel Multiple Unit on an excursion from Colne to Fleetwood for the Isle of Man. During single line working between Weeton and Singleton signal boxes, it crashed into a ballast train and jack-knifed into the air leaving seven dead.

Poulton-le-Fylde Station

Poulton station on the Preston & Wyre Railway main line to Fleetwood became a popular destination, despite the four mile road journey to the coast at Blackpool. On 29 April 1846 a branch line was opened to Blackpool with a triangular junction at Poulton. The sharp curve from the Preston side was so severe that a 6 mph speed limit was imposed by the Lancashire & Yorkshire Railway on its trains. However, London & North Western Railway trains had no speed restrictions at all in their Joint line regulations! Work had started to ease this curve in 1893 when the 11 pm LNWR Blackpool to Stockport express crashed at over 40 mph, killing two people.

The cut-off line was opened with the current station at Poulton on 5 April 1896, leaving the original site as a goods station on a spur. In 1899 another curve was laid to allow a direct link again from Blackpool to Fleetwood which was operated by steam railmotors. A halt survived here from 1909 to 1952 but this arm closed in 1964 while the original line to the goods station lasted until 1968. The double junction for Fleetwood remained in 1991 while the station was unique in keeping its canopy and all the buildings on the island platform, attractively restored.

Layton Station

Formerly known as Bispham, in 1857 this station first stood on the west side of a level crossing. It was rebuilt on the other side of the bridge which replaced the crossing. In July 1938 it was renamed Layton. On the skyline is Warbeck Water Tower, a reminder of the past problems of handling the vast peak season crowds. Water supplies to Central station were often restricted, so spare locomotive tenders were coupled together and taken to North station where supplies were more plentiful.

Blackpool North Station

The original station opened on 29 April 1846 with a building in the "Roman Ionic" style matching that at Lytham and one of the most imposing in the town. Yet traffic on the branch was so quiet for much of the year that the first stationmaster had time to run a farm at Layton as well, delivering milk in the mornings and parcels in the afternoons. The branch remained single track until growing pressure of visitors to the "Brighton of the North" led to it being doubled in 1865. The station, by then named Talbot Road, had become "uncomfortably crowded with spectators and idle people". By 1883 a goods shed alongside the two main platforms was used for excursion passengers.

The newly increased capacity of the main line with its fast lines and new signalling demanded a better terminus at Blackpool. In a two year operation finished in spring 1898, Talbot Road station was completely rebuilt and vastly enlarged. Behind the new entrance buildings there was a twin-arched overall roof covering the seven main platforms. A further eight open-air excursion platforms gave an aggregate length of almost two miles for trains, with a further 22 miles of carriage sidings beyond. At peak times, like August Bank Holiday 1910 when 229 trains brought 99,000 passengers, every siding in Poulton was used as well! The logistics of handling such numbers of passengers and trains have gone into legend.

Talbot Road was renamed Blackpool North in 1932 and a new concrete station canopy was opened in 1938 over the exposed circulating area for the excursion platforms. In January 1974 this formed the framework of the current Blackpool North station building. Meanwhile the tracks were lifted from the main platforms and the old roof and main building were demolished to permit the construction of a supermarket.

Top left: *The original Ionic style station at Blackpool Talbot Road was built in 1846 (photo: Evening Gazette).*

Top right: *The current Blackpool North station uses the framework of the 1938 Excursion shelter. Cars now park where tracks once led into the main station (photo: R. Kirkman).*

Bottom: *The 1898 trainshed at Talbot Road was cleared to build a supermarket (photo: Sankey collection).*

Opposite top: *Nine of the 17 excursion trains for over 10,000 workers at Bass Breweries in 1896. They are standing in the platforms currently used for Blackpool North station (photo: BR).*

Opposite bottom left: *Singleton box dated back to 1879. The station was a considerable distance from the village it served (photo: R. Kirkman).*

Opposite bottom right: *In 1990 BR Class 150 leaves Poulton-le-Fylde for Blackpool North, curving sharply left past No 3 box and the line to Burn Naze. The station retains all its awnings and buildings from 1896 (photo: P. van Zeller).*

Ex LMS Class 5 4-6-0s 45020 and 45045 start the Royal Train after an overnight stay in Poulton goods yard when the Queen visited Blackpool Opera House in 1955. These sidings were on the original alignment to Fleetwood, superseded by the route through the present station. Its gentler curve to Blackpool behind the locos was completed after the fatal derailment of 1893 (photo: Evening Gazette).

Burn Naze

The one-time main line to Fleetwood curves sharply at Poulton Junction and soon regains the old Preston & Wyre alignment. At Thornton for Cleveleys the barriers at the road crossing must be operated by train crew. The station opened as Cleveleys around 1870 and was rebuilt north of the road crossing in 1925, but closed in 1970. Currently only freight trains serve the ICI chemical works at Burn Naze. The plant was built near underground salt deposits and took regular block fuel and chemical trains through the five Hillhouse ground frames. To the north of Burn Naze there are few traces of the first line to Fleetwood which literally went to sea across two miles of narrow embankment and wooden trestle bridge. However, low funds and high tides stopped the hoped for land reclamation, and it was abandoned after a new alignment had been built in 1851 which gave a double track to Fleetwood.

Fleetwood

Sir Peter Hesketh-Fleetwood planned a major seaport here in conjunction with the P&WR. Decimus Burton planned the town with its North Euston Hotel, which still recalls when this was the northern terminus of the main line from London Euston. Although steamers sailed to Belfast, Ardrossan, Douglas and Barrow, the town grew slowly and trade was disappointing, hence the proposed docks were not opened until 8 October 1877. Designed by Sir John Hawkshaw they had eight miles of associated railway tracks and a huge grain store lettered Lancashire & Yorkshire Railway, the sponsors of the huge and costly project.

A new station was opened on the quayside on 16 July 1883 allowing direct access from trains into the boats for Belfast and Douglas. In 1885 a halt opened at Wyre Dock, where the fishing fleet was to become increasingly important. After the quayside station closed in 1966 a service ran to Wyre Dock, renamed Fleetwood, until the complete closure of the line to passengers in 1970. The rump to Wyre Dock Power Station closed in 1981 but an enthusiast group has relaid a short length of track.

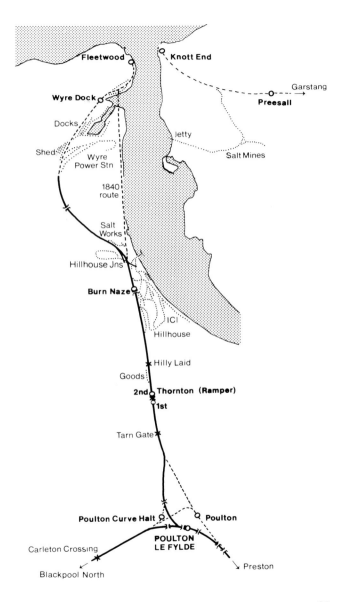

Top: *The vast grain elevator dominated Fleetwood docks long after its erection by the L&YR in 1882.*
Bottom: *Isle of Man Steam Packet Co SS Lady of Mann sailing out of the narrow Wyre channel for Douglas. Built in 1930 in the Company's centenary year, she operated the summer service to Fleetwood until 1971. A ship of the same name served the route in 1991 (both photos: P. van Zeller collection).*

"Lady of Mann" Outward Bound. Fleetwood.

Opposite top: *BR Derby built 2-car DMU approaches Fleetwood from Blackpool North on 7 August 1962. Close to the site of the P&WR terminus, the original route crossed the mudflats behind the front car to Burn Naze where the ICI plant now stands (photo: Frank Dean).*
Opposite bottom: *Class 47 193 Lucindae hauls an empty bulk fuel train in 1990 past Hillhouse sidings at ICI Burn Naze (photo: R. Kirkman).*

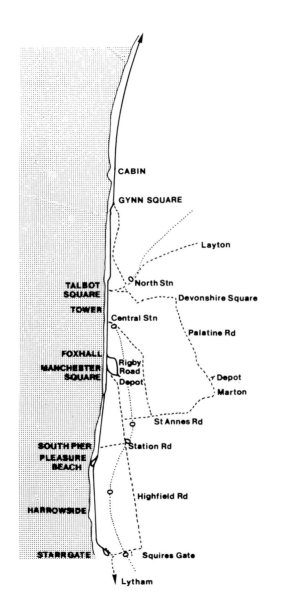

CABIN

GYNN SQUARE

Layton

North Stn

TALBOT
SQUARE

Devonshire Square

TOWER

Central Stn

Palatine Rd

FOXHALL

MANCHESTER
SQUARE

Rigby
Road
Depot

Depot

Marton

St Annes Rd

SOUTH PIER

Station Rd

PLEASURE
BEACH

Highfield Rd

HARROWSIDE

STARRGATE

Squires Gate

Lytham

Blackpool Tramways

The tramway along the seafront at Blackpool has kept alive the concept of the electric street railway. This was the first such line in the world and opened between Cocker Street and Station Road on 29 September 1885. The brainchild of Michael Holroyd Smith, it was first electrified with power conductors in a slot between the rails to avoid visual intrusion along the promenade. Alas, this conduit filled with water, and short circuits interfered with local railway signalling. The system was converted to overhead trolley wire in 1899 amid great controversy.

Talbot Square was the hub of the system, with tracks inland to Layton that closed in 1936 and Marton which lasted until 1962. However, the busiest section remains where the original route was moved in 1909, on the new promenade reserved track along The Golden Mile past the Tower. At Manchester Square, the junction into Lytham Road was opened in 1895 but now only gives access to the depot and works at Rigby Road, established in 1935.

The track opened further along the Promenade in 1903. The turning circle at Pleasure Beach is close to other sites of railway interest. A 15-inch gauge miniature railway was laid in 1905 by W.J. Bassett-Lowke but only lasted until 1909 because of the sandy conditions. In 1934 it was followed by the mile-long 21-inch gauge line built by Hudswell Clarke. Although this lost its Forth Bridge, its steam outline locomotives have been restored.

The southernmost section to Squires Gate was completed in 1926 and gave a further connection with the Lytham St. Annes Corporation Tramways. Lytham cars ran through to Blackpool until 28 April 1937, when like most British trams they were replaced by buses. Only the ability to move crowds along the reserved track on the promenade ensured the survival of the Blackpool trams to celebrate their centenary. In 1985 many trams including the first conduit car returned from the National Tramways Museum at Crich to run alongside the early Dreadnought and the new Jubilee double deck and Centenary single deck cars.

Opposite top: *Blackpool Electric Tramway Car 5 was the first in the world, built in 1885 by Lancaster Carriage & Wagon Co. It is loading at its northern terminus near Claremont Park. The underground electric supply was changed to overhead in 1899 (photo: Lancs County Libraries).*
Opposite bottom: *Centenary Car 644 was designed a century later to maintain all-year services along the promenade (photo: R. Kirkman).*
Right: *South Shore by the Pleasure Beach with two Railcoaches and an open "Boat" of Blackpool Corporation alongside a blue-and-white St Annes Corporation car. The latter through working ceased on 28 April 1937 (photo: R. Kirkman collection).*

PROMENADE SOUTH SHORE BLACKPOOL. B.G.1

43

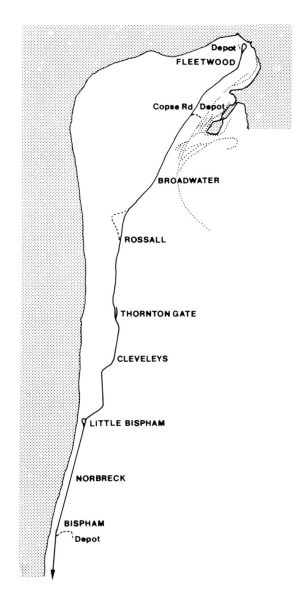

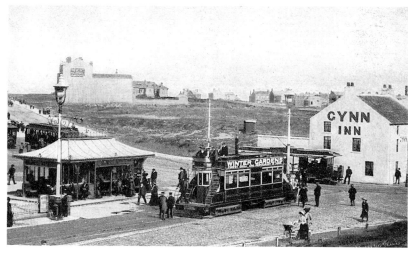

The Blackpool & Fleetwood Tramroad

The northern part of Blackpool's coast tramway was built by a separate company with a very different concept for an electric railway. The Blackpool & Fleetwood Tramroad followed American Interurban practice, using single deck cars (with overhead trolley wire) on railway track between towns to encourage suburban development. Its builders had just finished the 3-ft gauge Manx Electric Railway, and completed this 8-mile line in under 12 months for a formal opening on 30 July 1898. It was independent until 1 January 1920. It was absorbed by Blackpool Corporation Tramways, which then ran a freight service to Cleveleys until 1949. Improvements to the track and trams has kept bus competition at bay along the new road to Fleetwood. The route remains substantially intact apart from the depots and the street section from the old B&FT terminus at Talbot Road station to Gynn Square.

Here the tracks took to a private reservation for much of the route. The sharp curves on the promenade at Gynn Square show where the Corporation tramway was finally linked to the B&FT in 1922. This is also evident from the overhead poles which were between the B&FT tracks while the BCT erected its poles each side of the line.

The main stops are still called stations, like the Cabin where the tracks become a conventional fenced off railway, Bispham with its link to the old depot closed in 1966 and Thornton Gate with its permanent way sidings. This was the destination of coal trains from Fleetwood, with railway wagons hauled by the Tramway's electric locomotive. This is preserved with an original Tramroad open cross-bench car at The National Tramway Museum at Crich.

The original depot at Copse Road still stands with the B&FT monogram and 1897 Jubilee markings above the doors. Behind this was the link to Fleetwood railway yard. The final section of track ran down the middle of the street to terminate behind the North Euston Hotel. The present terminal loop by the Ferry to Knott End was laid in 1924 for the easier handling of trailer cars.

Lord's Quarry

Tootal Heights Quarry

New England Quarry

Longridge

Tunnel (40 yds)

Whittingham Hospital

○ **Grimsargh**

Ministry of Food

Red Scar

Ribbleton
(Gammer Lane)
(Fulwood)

Tramway

Lancaster

Blackpool

Oxheys

Brickworks

Greenbank
Siding

Deepdale

Mill St

862 yds

Deepdale St

Maudland
Bridge

PRESTON

Top left: *ex LBSCR 0-4-2 James Fryars and the "Sylum Billie" about to leave Grimsargh for Whittingham Hospital (photo: Lens of Sutton).*

Opposite: *ex LNWR G2 0-8-0 49451 running round at Longridge with a RCTS Mid Lancs Rail Tour on 22 September 1962. The loco obscures the station building which was attached to the Towneley Arms Hotel. The track continued in front of the loco to Tootal Heights Quarry (photo: Noel A. Machell).*

The Preston & Longridge Railway

This line was opened on 1 May 1840 to carry stone blocks from Tootal Heights Quarries to Preston for local municipal buildings and Liverpool Docks. The railway did not initially connect with other lines at Preston. It was worked by gravity from the quarries to Grimsargh, and from there by horse, as a clause in its Act required the consent of two JPs to use any steam locomotive!

The line was leased by the Fleetwood, Preston & West Riding Junction Railway which aimed to link Fleetwood with a proposed Blackburn, Clitheroe & North Western Junction Railway. The lessor company built the short section from the Preston & Wyre Railway at Maudlands Junction through three tunnels to the P&LR's Deepdale terminus. The two stations en route were described as "insignificant"! When however the FP&WRJR could not pay the rent it was taken over by the line it leased! Access to the Longridge line then involved reversal and a flat crossing over the Lancaster & Preston Junction Railway.

In June 1868 a short branch was laid as a private railway from Grimsargh to the Whittingham Hospital. It mainly moved coal and stores but carried passengers free. After the Longridge branch passenger service stopped on 2 June 1930, the "Sylum Billie" continued its free Saturday running for visitors until 29 June 1957.

In 1917 a Light Railway was authorised from Longridge to Hellifield but nothing came of it. After the branch closed to passengers, the quarries were rail connected until 1940. Freight trains continued to Longridge until 1967, after which they were progressively cut back. From 1938 to 1980 the Courtaulds factory at Red Scar was served by its own engines; one of these, *Caliban*, was rescued for the Lakeside & Haverthwaite Railway.

The final section of line in use is to the original Preston & Longridge terminus at Deepdale for bulk coal. Here shunting is still done by capstan, rope and gravity, recalling the original methods of working the P&LR.

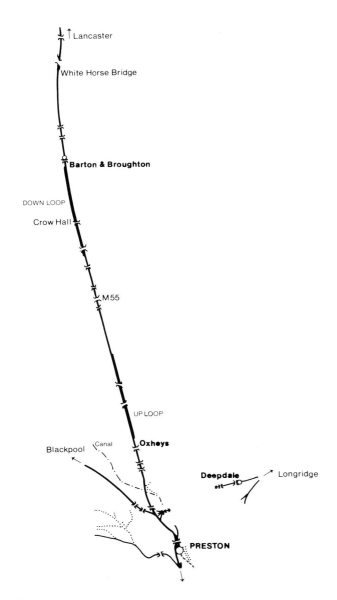

Greenbank Sidings and Oxheys

The Lancaster & Preston Junction Railway laid double track from the start. As traffic increased by 1903 two slow lines were added from Greenbank sidings to Barton & Broughton. The Greenbank Railway and its engines served an early industrial estate from 1881. After 1906 sidings were shunted by the main line company until closed in 1966. Oxheys sidings served the Preston Cattle Market. Before 1900 passenger trains stopped in both directions on the twice weekly market days, although by closure in 1925 only a platform on the up line to Preston was used.

Barton & Broughton

The L&PJR was remote from local communities, but found that the sentry boxes where the railway police acted as signalmen attracted passengers. Only a month after the line opened the directors ordered that even the first class and mail trains should stop at halts like Crow Hall. In November 1840 this moved to School Lane and even gained a short platform, being renamed Barton & Broughton in 1861. Although closed to passengers on 1 May 1939, the stone L&PJR station building survives on the down side overlooking the LNWR brick buildings on the old platform. Barton Viaduct carries the line over the Barton Brook on three stone and brick arches.

White Horse Tunnel

This bridge proved a major problem to the contractors as the line could not force the turnpike (now the A6) to deviate. They had to build an expensive skew bridge instead. The line should have opened on 8 June 1840 but only days before the bridge collapsed — workmen had been "most improperly pounding some puddle right on top of the newly turned arch". It was quickly rebuilt for the opening on 25 June but fell in again two weeks later! Passengers had to walk over the rubble until the line was reopened. After these early problems the structures of the L&PJR survived weights and speeds of trains far beyond what their builders could conceive, until the alterations to carry the overhead wiring erected in 1973.

Top: *LMS 4-6-2 6224 Princess Alexandra in blue and silver takes water at Brock troughs with the Up Coronation Scot on 18 August 1939. Replicas of the badger emblems were restored on this and another local bridge when it was rebuilt for electrification (photo: Frank Dean).*

Right: *BR Class 150 passing the former L&PJR station building at Barton and Broughton (photo: R. Kirkman).*

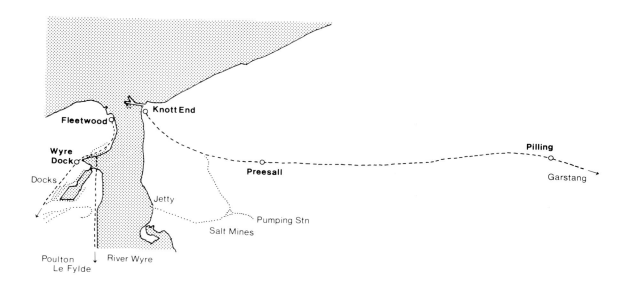

Garstang & Knott End Railway

An early tramway proposal to Garstang was turned into a major railway scheme to link the east coast with a port on the Wyre estuary opposite Fleetwood. Misspent funds meant the Garstang & Knott End Railway was only built as far as Pilling on 5 December 1870, and could not afford even to buy rolling stock. With fortunes revived by a receiver, the trains took their nickname of "The Pilling Pig" from the whistle of a new locomotive, *Farmers' Friend*.

At length a new company was formed in 1898 to finish the line and extend it towards Lancaster. After yet another decade the line to Knott End was completed, and the old company merged with the new. Traffic came from a saltworks at Preesall until a pipeline was built under the Wyre to the Burn Naze works near Fleetwood. On 29 March 1930 the last passenger train was an ex-London & North Western Railway steam railcar. On 13 November 1950 the last goods train worked right through to Knott End.

Garstang & Catterall

Garstang station was some distance from the town which was better served by the Lancaster Canal packet boats. To tempt customers on to rails, the L&PJR made a new road and put on a free horse-bus service to the station. Even with a new name, the station was no nearer to Catterall!

When the Garstang & Knott End Railway opened on 5 December 1870, its trains used the west side of the down island platform. Its track ran alongside the main line for almost a mile, within the now empty arches in the over bridges north of Garstang, before branching west into a shallow cutting. Freight continued to use the branch until 1965, while Garstang & Catterall station closed on 3 February 1969. All railway buildings and platforms were removed by 1972 and the site now supplies power from the National Grid for the 25kV ac 50 cycles overhead electric catenary on this section of main line.

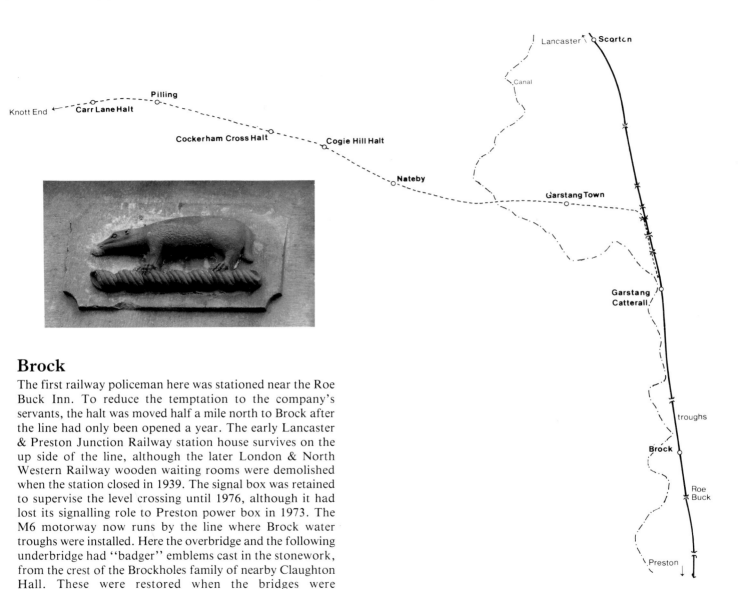

Brock

The first railway policeman here was stationed near the Roe Buck Inn. To reduce the temptation to the company's servants, the halt was moved half a mile north to Brock after the line had only been opened a year. The early Lancaster & Preston Junction Railway station house survives on the up side of the line, although the later London & North Western Railway wooden waiting rooms were demolished when the station closed in 1939. The signal box was retained to supervise the level crossing until 1976, although it had lost its signalling role to Preston power box in 1973. The M6 motorway now runs by the line where Brock water troughs were installed. Here the overbridge and the following underbridge had "badger" emblems cast in the stonework, from the crest of the Brockholes family of nearby Claughton Hall. These were restored when the bridges were reconstructed for electrification.

Top left: *The last pick up goods train from Knott End left behind BR Class 2 2-6-0 46429. Last rites were celebrated by local railwaymen on 13 November 1950 (photo: Evening Gazette).*
Top right: *Garstang Town Station with Hudswell Clarke 0-6-0 Jubilee Queen and an original G&KER coach circa 1900.*
Bottom right: *Manning Wardle 0-6-0 Knott End takes one of the first trains out of Knott End in 1908, with signalling works in progress (photos: Lens of Sutton).*

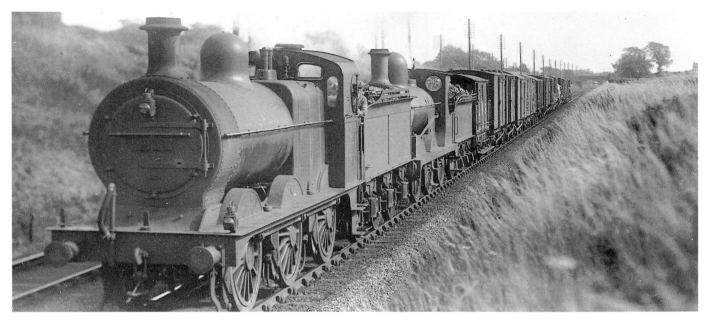

Top: *ex MR Deeley 3231 and ex L&YR Aspinall 12225 3F 0-6-0s double head a northbound freight on the L&PJR towards Lancaster in the 1930s (photo: R. Kirkman collection).*
Bottom: *The Premier line with an immaculate LNWR 0-8-0 on a freight near Galgate before the Great War (photo: Sir Aubrey Brocklebank).*

Scorton

Scorton police box was also moved to the site of the later station. There was no goods yard and its signal box was replaced by intermediate block signals before the station closed in 1930. Scorton has now lost all traces of its station. The six-arch Wyre viaduct carries the line over the road and river. Although there were few major structures, the Lancaster & Preston Junction Railway cost over £400,000, much more than was estimated by Joseph Locke. As traffic receipts were low, the Board quickly leased the line first to the competing Canal and then to the Lancaster & Carlisle Railway. When the Canal refused to give up its rights, the L&PJR found itself in an extraordinary mess with local trains run by the Canal and expresses by the L&CR!

Bay Horse

The LNWR station house and goods shed remain where this halt took its name from an inn. However, it was the site of an infamous accident in 1848 when a L&CR locomotive with a Euston-Glasgow express ran into a stationary L&PJR local train. The Railway Inspector who investigated the affair stated, "So many causes combined to produce this catastrophe that it is not easy to determine to which to give precedence"! The L&PJR train had run out of steam. The express was late and had set off only five minutes behind, trying to make up time even though there was another train ahead. The only signal at Bay Horse was a flag wrapped tightly round its post by the wind!

Galgate

This station had no sidings and the signal box closed by 1905. After complete closure in 1939, the remaining buildings vanished prior to electrification. Overlooking Galgate basin on the canal, the line runs across another skew bridge over the turnpike which gave problems in construction. The viaduct of six 30ft arches over the River Conder and the road was the greatest engineering work along the line. The first stone was laid on Queen Victoria's Coronation Day 28 June 1838, and several Victoria Medals were deposited under it.

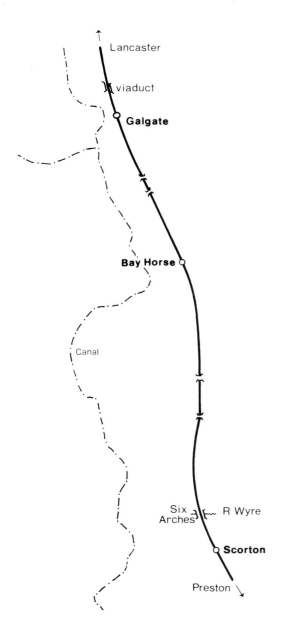

Lancaster

viaduct

Galgate

Bay Horse

Canal

Six Arches   R Wyre

Scorton

Preston

150 years after the opening of the
L&PJR, many of its structures still
form part of the main line of 1990.
Top: Network Northwest Class 150
from Manchester to Barrow crosses
the line's old rival, the Lancaster
Canal at the bottom of Ripley
Bank.
Bottom: Class 90 hauls a Glasgow-
Birmingham over Galgate viaduct.
Opposite top: Class 90 038 speeds
under White Horse skew bridge
(photos: P. van Zeller).
Opposite bottom: Class 86 404
crosses Six Arches viaduct near
Scorton (photo: R. Kirkman).

Lancaster Old Junction

The sharp curve with its speed restriction from 110 to 75 mph was where the Lancaster & Carlisle Railway joined the original route of the Lancaster & Preston Junction Railway half a mile outside its Penny Street terminus. This opened on 25 June 1840 but closed on 1 August 1849 after both lines were amalgamated. The main Georgian style building with its entrance portico was sold and survives as a nurses' home overlooking the canal. The site then became a goods station until 1967.

Lancaster No 1 signalbox was sited by the junction with the L&CR. Opposite was Ripley engine shed which replaced an earlier structure in 1875. It had a small allocation of 11 locomotives in 1925 but closed in 1934. The Ripley bank descending at 1 in 98 into Lancaster was formerly the site for a Post Office Travelling Mail pick-up apparatus.

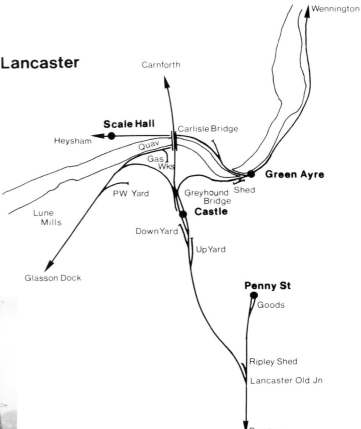

Lancaster

Opposite: *ex LMS 8P 4-6-2 46229 Duchess of Hamilton storms up the 1 in 98 over the trap points on Ripley Bank with an afternoon Glasgow-Birmingham on 14 April 1962 (photo: Noel A. Machell).*
Left: *LNWR 2-2-2 Engineer Lancaster, formerly L&CR No 39 Canning built at Crewe in 1857, stands at Ripley Shed before scrapping in 1903. The shed lay between the L&CR and the L&PJR (photo: Lancaster City Museum).*

Lancaster Castle Station

The original L&CR station survives in the gothic style buildings on the main down No 3 platform where one of the chimneys still carries the initials L&C. The station was extended in 1856, but the present layout is the result of the major remodelling completed in 1902. This gave two fast through lines and No 6 platform for Midland Railway connecting services. These took the sharply curved and falling grade around the Castle and Priory church. At the end of bay platforms 1 and 2 on the west side of the station was the junction for the quayside and Glasson Dock branches. The whole of the north end of the station was controlled by the Lancaster No 4 signal box. This tall type 6 box, which had an impressive 144 levers, opened in 1901 and closed in 1973.

Opposite top left: *At Lancaster, BR Class 7 4-6-2 70045 Lord Rowallan starts south in 1966, past semaphore signals and a full goods yard.*
Opposite top right: *A Driving Van Trailer leads a southbound express at the same place 25 years later (both photos: P. van Zeller).*
Opposite bottom left: *BR Class 142 with Network Northwest logos rolls into Lancaster. The chimney behind the overhead mast still bears the L & C monogram (photo: R. Kirkman).*

Below: *ex LMS class 5 4-6-0 45347 runs into Platform 4 at Lancaster Castle with a local passenger train. The track layout with its fast lines has survived but both rolling stock and signalling have changed in 25 years. A Morecambe train waits in the bay. The line to Glasson Dock swung sharply round the gasometer past No 4 Signal Box. The electric overhead wiring from the Green Ayre branch then only served Platforms 5 and 6 (photo: John M. Hammond).*

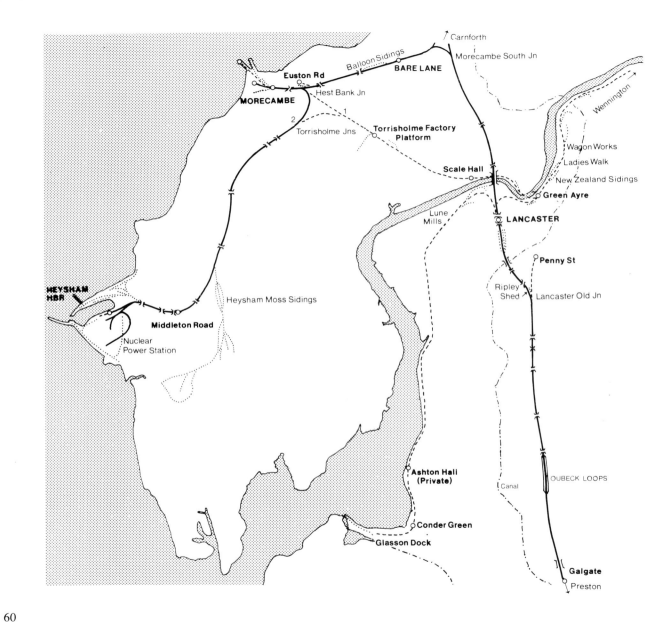

Carnforth

Balloon Sidings

BARE LANE

Morecambe South Jn

Euston Rd

Hest Bank Jn

MORECAMBE

Wennington

2

1

Torrisholme Jns

Torrisholme Factory
Platform

Wagon Works

Ladies Walk

New Zealand Sidings

Scale Hall

Green Ayre

Lune
Mills

LANCASTER

HEYSHAM
HBR

Penny St

Ripley
Shed

Lancaster Old Jn

Heysham Moss Sidings

Middleton Road

Nuclear
Power Station

OUBECK LOOPS

Ashton Hall
(Private)

Canal

Conder Green

Glasson Dock

Galgate

Preston

Glasson Dock Branch

Lancaster was a major port until the River Lune became silted. The dock at Glasson had been completed in 1791 and connected to the Lancaster Canal in 1826. Although a railway had long been proposed, the branch was not opened until 9 July 1883. It included sidings on to St George's Quay. The Williamson's linoleum factory had its own 3 ft gauge internal works line on to the quay, served by two Dick Kerr 0-4-0s. A station at Ashton Hall was the private halt of Lord Ashton who owned the factory.

However, freight traffic only briefly flourished before the opening of Heysham Harbour when Spanish ore was being imported for Carnforth Ironworks. From the 1920s two LNWR steam railcars worked services from a depot at Lancaster Bridge Road. However, passenger services were abandoned in 1930. Freight continued until September 1964, while the quayside lines lasted a further five years.

Green Ayre Branch

The North Western Railway opened its link to Lancaster Castle station on 19 December 1849, shortly after its line from Morecambe to Lancaster Green Ayre was extended to Wennington. Passenger services were suspended from 1876 but were restored in 1881 and even electrified in 1908. A derailment occurred on the sharp curve near the station in 1962. Passenger services closed on 3 January 1966 but freight trains continued to have access to factories and Lancaster Power Station at Ladies Walk sidings until 17 March 1976. The fireless steam locomotives at the old power station were transferred to the Heysham nuclear plant. Lancaster Green Ayre engine shed site became a supermarket and the Greyhound bridge across the Lune a road bridge.

Carlisle Bridge

The problems of crossing the River Lune at Lancaster led the first railway proposals to avoid the town. A petition from 228 citizens supported a Deviation Act, but the L&CR had to improve the river navigation before the Admiralty would allow it to cross at this point. It was "a stupendous construction" to raise eight stone and three great laminated timber spans from the main stone piers. These had 30,000 cu ft of timber but only twenty years later required complete replacement by wrought-iron girders. In 1962-3 the bridge was again rebuilt but without interrupting either rail or the statutory foot traffic. The new main girders were hoisted out from the quayside on a monorail. Then the running tracks were interlaced to allow concrete beams to be poured on each side of the bridge, which still uses the original piers.

BR Class 2 2-6-0 46441 nears Condor Green with the last railtour to Glasson Dock on 20 June 1964. The loco was preserved at Steamtown (photo: Noel A. Machell).

Opposite top: *The first bridge over the Lune at Lancaster was "a stupendous construction" with its three laminated timber arches. The piers still support the West Coast main line. The overgrown (little) North Western Railway to Morecambe had a station under one arch (photo: Lancaster City Museum).*
Opposite bottom: *ex LMS Class 5 4-6-0 45323 crosses the newly rebuilt Carlisle Bridge on 30 November 1963 with a Burn Naze to Whitehaven anhydrite train (photo: Noel A. Machell).*

Above: *ex LMS Fowler 3F 0-6-0T "Jinty" 47531 drifts down from Lancaster Castle to Green Ayre on 25 September 1964 under the timber Midland Railway overhead supports. These trip workings survived closure of the through route from Morecambe to Wennington to supply coal to Lancaster Power Station until 1976. The 1910 Greyhound Bridge in the background remains as a road link (photo: Noel A. Machell).*

Morecambe

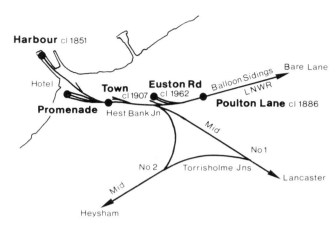

Morecambe Promenade Station

The seaside town of Morecambe did not exist when the potential of the coast drew the [little] North Western Railway to plan a deep water port and build a wooden pier. Passenger trains ran on to the stone jetty from 1852 to connect with steamers to Belfast and Douglas. Goods trains lasted until 1933, latterly serving shipbreakers using the harbour. The original station and lighthouse survives, used by Morecambe Bay Fisheries.

After the Midland Railway takeover, the station at Northumberland Road was rebuilt in 1872, but was later superseded by the current Promenade station on 24 March 1907. In 1991 this retained four platforms, Art Nouveau decoration and a vast gentlemen's urinal, although most modern trains were only two-car diesel multiple units.

The London & North Western Railway used the Midland station before 1886. It then opened its own station at Euston Road close to the point of connection with the Midland, and closed its Poulton Lane station. Although never of the magnitude of Blackpool, traffic to Morecambe during the Illuminations could fill every platform and siding available. However, after only opening in the summer from 1958, Euston Road closed completely in 1962.

Heysham Harbour Station

Heysham Harbour was opened by the MR in 1904 for its Belfast and Isle of Man sailings which had earlier used the Furness Railway docks at Barrow in Furness. From 1898 a new line from Morecambe gave access to the 350 acre site for construction. In a £3m scheme the harbour was first excavated, then flooded. Torrisholme triangle allowed direct access for trains from London St Pancras, although trains from Green Ayre reversed at Morecambe.

The 40 ft deep Heysham Channel allowed access at all states of the tide. In 1928 sailings from Fleetwood were transferred to Heysham and boat trains from London and Manchester then used the LNWR route with a reversal at Morecambe Promenade. Northern Ireland traffic fell during the Troubles and, although a new station was only opened on 4 May 1970, it closed on 6 October 1975. After the loss of Irish traffic, a new Manx Line service to Douglas began in 1978. When this merged with the Isle of Man Steam Packet Company, the daily sailings from Liverpool were transferred to Heysham. Boat trains were reintroduced in the 1987 summer season. Freight traffic was enhanced by oil and chemical traffic until the 1970s when construction began on the nuclear power stations. These now have rail access and two fireless steam locomotives.

Opposite top: *An LNWR 0-6-2T Coal Tank arrives at Morecambe Euston Road (photo: Lens of Sutton).*
Opposite bottom: *In 1990 remnants of electrification at Morecambe overshadowed BR Class 143 in Metro Train livery. It ran the boat trains to Heysham before returning to Leeds via Lancaster (photo: P. van Zeller).*
Top: *Heysham Harbour was excavated from dry land using both steam navvies and horse power from 1898-1904 (photo: Lancaster City Museum).*
Bottom: *SS Duke of Rothesay at the South Quay at Heysham. This boat started sailing to Belfast in 1927 when Fleetwood sailings were transferred (photo: R. Kirkman collection).*

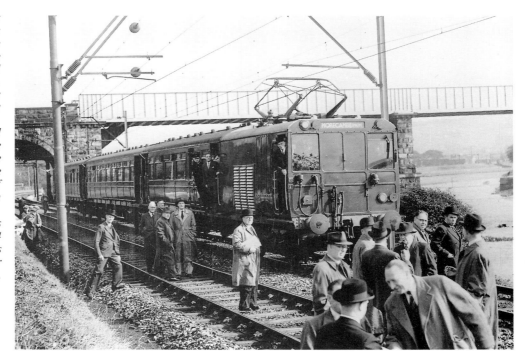

Right: *In 1953 a 3-car set of ex LNWR stock stands while officials of English Electric, BICC and the Railway Executive inspect "the Golden Mile" of overhead equipment for future 25Kv lines. Carlisle bridge is in its intermediate state (photo: Lancaster City Museum).*

Opposite top: *Overhead wires and signal gantries guard the approaches to Morecambe Promenade in 1908. In 1991 these tracks faced cutback to the site of Northumberland Street Station (photo: R. Kirkman collection).*

Opposite bottom: *M28219M leaves Heysham on 25 September 1964 past Harbour Junction box. Tracks still divide here for the Nuclear Power stations (photo: Noel A. Machell).*

Lancaster-Morecambe-Heysham Electrification

The MR decided to electrify the lines between Lancaster, Morecambe and Heysham using power generated at the port power station in a building which still stands. 6,600V ac current was supplied to overhead wires supported by cross girders on timber posts and earthed into the Greyhound viaduct at Lancaster. The new services were introduced in the summer of 1908. They used new power cars and trailers in sets which could be strengthened by adding ordinary coaches with control cables fastened to the footsteps. The route involved two reversals at Green Ayre and Morecambe, but it worked successfully until February 1951 when steam auto trains were introduced.

The line was converted from 6,600V ac at 25 cycles to 50 cycles to test equipment for proposed main-line high-voltage electrification schemes taking power from the national grid at 25,000V ac 50 cycles. It reopened on 17 August 1953 using three-car sets built in 1914 for the LNWR Willesden-Earls Court line. To test equipment for future main-line electrification schemes, each set had different fittings, including one with a Faiverley pantograph. Four thousand feet of track alongside the River Lune had a variety of new prototype catenary supports including a "tunnel" and was nicknamed "The Golden Mile". Close by a new station was opened at Scale Hall on 8 June 1957. The line had trains every 15 minutes on summer Saturdays but closed on 3 January 1966 along with passenger services through Lancaster Green Ayre to Wennington Junction.

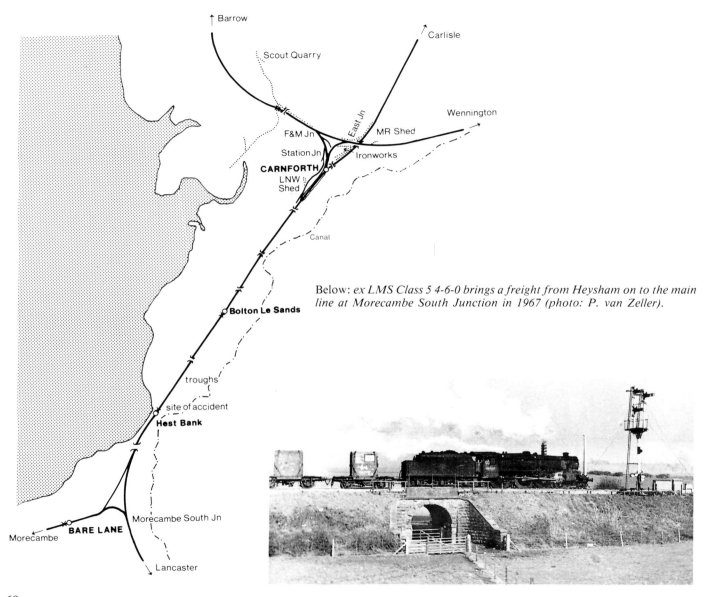

↑ Barrow

Carlisle

Scout Quarry

F&M Jn

East Jn

MR Shed

Wennington

Station Jn

Ironworks

CARNFORTH

LNW
Shed

Canal

○ **Bolton Le Sands**

troughs

site of accident

Hest Bank

Morecambe South Jn

Morecambe ← ○ **BARE LANE**

Lancaster

Below: *ex LMS Class 5 4-6-0 brings a freight from Heysham on to the main line at Morecambe South Junction in 1967 (photo: P. van Zeller).*

Morecambe South Junction — Bare Lane Station

The direct route to the Morecambe branch from Morecambe South Junction was not built until May 1888. It was then a double track junction until it was singled in 1988 to eliminate the diamond crossing. At Bare Lane station the single track met the first route from the main line into Morecambe. This and Poulton Lane Halt opened on 8 August 1864. The London & North Western Railway used the North Western Railway terminus at Northumberland Road until it built its own station at Euston Road in 1886.

Hest Bank and Bolton-le-Sands Level Crossings

The original Morecambe branch was the single line which follows the main line before the junction at Hest Bank. It was hoped that Durham coke coming over the Stainmore route could be exported from Morecambe so the LNWR laid double track, but this was soon singled. Later, Midland Railway locomotives had running powers to take iron ore from Heysham Harbour to the ironworks at Carnforth.

The original Lancaster & Carlisle Railway station house and crossing keepers' cottage survived the closure of the station in February 1969. In the 1930s there was a unique windmill which generated electricity for the station. Now there is a windspeed indicator to warn Preston power box to restrict the speed of trains when crosswinds over 65 mph endanger the overhead wires.

The British Railways box of 1958 was kept as a level crossing gate box after the 1973 resignalling, and since 1977 has also controlled the level crossing barriers at Bolton-le-Sands 1½ miles away. This station also opened in 1849 and closed in 1969. Between these two crossings a 20 ft deep peat bog took thousands of tons of material during construction of the line. Close to Hest Bank were the water troughs which saw a major accident on 20 May 1962. A broken rail derailed all coaches of the Glasgow-Kensington sleeper at 70 mph but without any fatalities.

Carnforth

The first L&CR station opened here in 1846 as Carnforth-Yealand. The original building on the down platform was considerably extended in 1857 for trains from the Ulverstone & Lancaster Railway. Shortly after the U&LR was taken over by the Furness Railway, the Furness & Midland Junction Railway was completed from Wennington in 1867. Midland Railway trains ran directly towards Barrow at F&M Junction where there were briefly two stations.

In 1880 a triangle brought MR trains to terminate in the bay of a new station. Jointly owned by the LNWR and the FR, it had an extensive overall roof supported by brackets bearing the initials of the two companies. The FR trains in both directions used one long face of a triangular platform to exchange passengers with the other companies. An old FR signal box still stands on the platform end bearing its carved company crest.

Carnforth grew in importance when its ironworks opened in 1867. This occupied a site between the triangle and the LNWR main line and had a private tramway to Scout quarry and slagbanks on the shore. In 1940 the station was given a new down Furness line platform distinguished by its concrete architecture. It remains in use for trains to Barrow and Leeds, while the LNWR platforms closed in May 1970 and were fenced off for safety.

Steamtown

The three companies had their own sheds until the 1923 grouping when they were centralised on the LNWR shed. Following the major rebuilding of the station, a new locomotive depot was built on the site of the old FR shed with a tall coaling tower. It was one of the last British Rail sheds to keep steam locomotives until August 1968. Local enthusiasts hoped it could be the support base for the Lakeside branch preserved in its entirety. It reopened as a steam centre in its own right, with standard gauge and 15in gauge running tracks along the length of the old marshalling yard. It has serviced steam locomotives to work over the Settle-Carlisle and Cumbrian Coast routes.

Opposite top: *ex LMS Class 5 4-6-0 45399 takes a Heysham to Carnforth trip freight through Bare Lane on 11 October 1964 (photo: Noel A. Machell).*

Opposite bottom: *ex LMS Co-Co 10000 and 10001 double-heading the down Royal Scot, working wrong line at Morecambe South Junction on 15 June 1957 (photo: Noel A. Machell).*

Top: *BR Class 90 016 leading a DVT past Hest Bank Junction. The L&CR station-house still stands next to the level crossing (photo: P. van Zeller).*

Bottom: *LNWR Precedent class 2-4-0 at the same place 90 years earlier (photo: Lancaster City Museum).*

Opposite: *ex LMS Class 5 4-6-0 44875 at Carnforth with a Morecambe-Leeds train in 1967 (photo: P. van Zeller).*

Bottom: *BR 1Co-Co1 English Electric Type 4 D303 pulls past Carnforth No 1 Junction box with the 6.30pm Kendal to Kilburn parcel train on 15 May 1963. These locos were about to take over the work of the Stanier Pacifics (photo: Noel A. Machell).*